Visiting Picasso

Visiting Picasso

Poems by Jim Barnes

University of Illinois Press
Urbana and Chicago

Library of Congress Cataloging-in-Publication Data

Barnes, Jim, 1933–

Visiting Picasso : poems / by Jim Barnes.

p. cm.

ISBN-13: 978-0-252-03129-8 (acid-free paper)

ISBN-10: 0-252-03129-6 (acid-free paper)

ISBN-13: 978-0-252-07373-1 (pbk. : acid-free paper)

ISBN-10: 0-252-07373-8 (pbk. : acid-free paper)

I. Title.

PS3552.A67395V57   2007

811'.54--dc22   2006029930

Contents

Homage to Nabokov / 1

Leaving Chillon / 2

L'Exposition / 3

Charlie and the Funicular / 4

Waiting for Recognition / 6

Remembering Cap Canaille / 8

Always Completely at Home / 9

In Cassis, Early March / 10

In Vauvenargues / 12

Gwawdodyns for the Fisher King / 13

Rue du Faubourg St.-Honoré / 14

Ballade / 17

Weather / 19

The Poetry Reading near La Californie after a Day on
    Golfe Juan / 21

The Judgment of Paris (Whereabouts Unknown) / 22

Watching TV at Dooley's, the Early 1950s / 24

Zen / 25

Winter's End, 1970 / 26

Sibyl / 28

Féria de Pâques, Arles 1996 / 29

The American Heritage Potato / 31

Postcard to Andrew Grossbardt from the Confluence of the
  Fourche Maline and Holson Creek, Summerfield,
  Oklahoma, 1 September 1975 / 32

By the Ruins / 33

Postcard to David Ray from Poteau Mountain, Runestone
  State Park / 34

Corniche de l'Estérel / 35

The Artist as Beachcomber / 37

Picture of Creeley, Rediscovered after Hearing Him Read
  in Munich, February 1995 / 38

A Book of the Dead / 39

Winter's End / 40

Fin de Siècle at Schloss Solitude / 42

Birkenkopf 1998 / 44

These Flat-Topped Pines Crouch / 45

In St.-Maximin-Ste.-Baume with the Old Men at *Boules*,
  Looking for the Maestro / 46

Deputy Finds Dean's Tombstone on Highway / 48

Epitaph for J(ohn). B(erryman). / 50

Monsieur le Marquis de Vauvenargues / 51

The Marsh Bird / 54

The Cave on Cavanal Mountain / 55

Portrait in Seven Parts with Nightscape / 56

Heading East Out of Rock Springs / 58

Birkenkopf 2000 / 60

Giuseppe's Song for His Annelise / 61

The Fox at Agay / 62

Visiting Picasso / 63

La Vieille Madame à la Machine à Sous / 65

Rubaiyat for a Pair of Heroes / 67

On the Hill Back of La Ciotat   /   68

Ithaka 2001   /   69

Lay   /   71

The First Féria of the Third Millennium, Arles Easter
    Monday   /   72

In Aix-en-Provence   /   74

The Poet's Paradise   /   76

Agamemnon   /   77

The Snow Bird   /   79

Twister   /   80

Ikaros 1940   /   81

Owl   /   83

Rondeau for a Shovelbill Catfish, at the Buffalo Hole,
    Fourche Maline River, à la Research du Temps Perdu,
    January 2003   /   84

Magpie   /   85

West of Cassis   /   86

Taos as Purgatory   /   87

Epithalamion: Villanelle for September 7, 2002   /   88

In Memory of Dora Maar   /   89

Elegy for the Old Man beside the Road to Nans les Pins   /   90

Villa Serbelloni Revisited, February 2003   /   91

Acknowledgments

Most of the poems first appeared in literary magazines, and grateful acknowledgment is therefore made to the editors of the following:

The World and I for "Homage to Nabokov," "L'Exposition," and "Charlie and the Funicular"
The Georgia Review for "Leaving Chillon"
The Carriage House Review for "Waiting for Recognition"
Poetry (Chicago) for "Remembering Cap Canaille"
88: A Journal of Contemporary American Poetry for "Always Completely at Home"
The Mid-America Poetry Review for "In Cassis, Early March" and "Sibyl,"
Arts & Letters: Journal of Contemporary Culture for "In Vauvenargues," and "Fin de Siècle at Schloss Solitude"
Nebraska Review for "Gwawdodyns for the Fisher King"
Great River Review for "Rue du Faubourg St.-Honoré," "Monsieur le Marquis de Vauvenargues," and "The Artist as Beachcomber"
The Phoenix Review (Australia) for "The Poetry Reading near La Californie after a Day on Golfe Juan" (under the title "The Reading")
South Dakota Review for "Watching TV at Dooley's, the Early 1950s"
Runes: A Review of Poetry for "Zen"
The New Laurel Review for "Winter's End, 1970"
Colorado Review for "Féria de Pâques, Arles 1996"
Luna for "Postcard to Andrew Grossbardt from the Confluence of the Fourche Maline and Holson Creek, Summerfield, Oklahoma, 1 September 1975" and "Portrait in Seven Parts with Nightscape"
CutBank for "By the Ruins" (under the title "On Blue Mountain Tower")

Invisible City for "Postcard to David Ray from Poteau Mountain, Runestone State Park"

Poetry Northwest for "Corniche de l'Estérel"

Oakwood for "Picture of Creeley, Rediscovered after Hearing Him Read in Munich, February 1995" (under another form) and "The Cave on Cavanal Mountain"

Tendril for "A Book of the Dead"

Amicus Journal for "Winter's End"

The American Scholar for "Deputy Finds Dean's Tombstone on Highway"

Tar River Review for "Epitaph for J(ohn). B(erryman)."

Green River Review for "The Marsh Bird," "Owl," and "Magpie"

Boulevard for "The Fox at Agay"

Sewanee Review for "Visiting Picasso" and "The First Féria of the Third Millennium, Arles Easter Monday"

The Formalist for "La Vieille Madame à la Machine à Sous" and "On the Hill Back of La Ciotat"

The North American Review for "Ithaka 2001"

River City for "In Aix-en-Provence"

Prairie Schooner for "These Flat-Topped Pines Crouch"

River Styx for "The Poet's Paradise"

The Nation for "The Snow Bird"

Aspect for "Twister"

University of Portland Review for "Ikaros 1940" (under the title "First Flight")

Skree for "Taos as Purgatory"

The Gingko Tree Review for "In Memory of Dora Maar," "Elegy for the Old Man Beside the Road to Nans les Pins," "Rubaiyat for a Pair of Heroes," and "West of Cassis"

The Chariton Review for "Villa Serbelloni Revisited, February 2003"

The poems "In Vauvenaragues" and "Sibyl" appear in *Ghosts: An Anthology* (Helicon Nine Editions, 2005). The poem "The American Heritage Potato" appears in *Spud Songs* (Helicon Nine Editions, 1997). In addition, the poems "Féria de Pâques, Arles 1996," "By the Ruins," "Winter's End," "West of Cassis," and "Watching TV at Dooley's, the Early 1950s" appear in *The First Abbeywood Anthology: Wings and Waking Dreams* (Abbeywood Press, 2007).

Special thanks to the Camargo Foundation and its executive director, Michael Pretina, for the two spring semester-long fellowships, in 1996 and 2001, during which time many of the poems in this volume were written.

Also, special thanks to the Rockefeller Foundation Bellagio Conference Center and its executive director, Gianna Celli, for a month-long fellowship (February 2003), during which time several of the poems were written.

Homage To Nabokov

The day is sharp with blades of wind thrown down
from the Bernese Alps, the glinting sun cruel
in its insistence upon an icy shine.
Today nothing happens above Montreux
except the roiling clouds and Norway pines
whose heavy limbs speak of memory in lieu
of snow. Yet, as we enter the gate, the sound

of song flows down the hill from the gray fold
of Châtelard, where hands are pruning vines. Black
granite slab, a black stone lettered in gold,
the one last name. We come too late to ask
your pardon for the letter I sent, my old
request for your contribution, to which
Véra answered curtly, in type bolder

than my Royal's had been, that VN did not
send things for consideration. Too late
we know humility and the aching rot
of pride. Forgive me for my once rude state
of imbecility: indeed I did not
know your life. We hand you the wrinkled fruit
from the persimmon tree, its flesh a hot

pale fire on our tongues. There is no great risk
in eating the fruit in this graveyard: the frost
of November has cooked the skins and mist
from Evian has washed them clean. At most
we will stay an hour and feel we are blessed
to have leaned upon your good name, a host
of vines at our backs, and made our visit.

1

Leaving Chillon

Something dark stays with you on leaving the Château
de Chillon, not the memory of Byron's name
graved on the column where Bonnivard was chained below
nor the fog that rides the surface of the lake. The lame
gatekeeper gives you the evil eye when you go
past the stile and leave no Swiss francs. Not the same
dark that you know from deep night but the dark of threat
that is dreamed palpable. The history of sweat

and blood, the prisoner chained for years, the holy war
between the towns—all this falls away. But the stark weight
of Chillon bends your back for miles along the shore.
You try to shake it from your thoughts, consider shades
of trees at water's edge, or roses that are more
at bloom than you have ever seen up the brick way
to Villa Isabelle. The monkey trees and palms
are darkly green, and at gloaming Lac Léman is calm

in the growing fog. You speak and try to calm your mind.
No one is near except the birds. You say a verse
or two from Byron's poem, something like *strove to rend
my bonds,* and stop. You have lost nothing here from first
to last visit. All is fictive, a sham of mind
you walk into along this promenade. The birds
are quacking at your loss of sense. Dark in low flight,
Chillon hangs above the lake, below the coming night.

L'Exposition

A cold day in Martigny
and we come to see the work
of Marie Laurencin. Her
portraits blur into form, lurk

oriental and light. Some-
thing dark from the eyes holds us.
The pastels are smooth as dream,
the brush she used cream to touch.

All the eyes seem oval slants,
all the robes leant by the gods
long absent from this Celtic
place Romans built on. The road

in named us native as scree
above our heads. We feel stone
threaten the figures that her
light touch turned into a tone

that is hers alone, but know
that the flow of color will
remain glacial and frozen
into forms that open still.

Charlie and the Funicular

Rare December day: the sun breaks
into a radiance over Alps
few are witness to. The perched clog
car is almost empty. Knees ache
from the altitude and cobble-
stones. After over a mile up

you feel a need for valleys, fields
of grain and butterflies. Charlie
Chaplin lies far below. You can
barely see Clarens. My head reels
with a dizziness comic and free
as a tramp in spring. Vevey and

Montreux are spread along the lake
under blue haze. If Chaplin were
here, the line would break, the clog wheel
slip from greased cups, and we would take
one hell of a ride back down to where
we started from, alive and well,

no worse at all for the fast fall down,
except hats gone and shirttails in
the wind. Funny how you can think
death would pass you by if and when
this or that were real. We begin
the descent and feel our hearts sink

at the thought that death could happen,
that indeed it eventually would,
in some form, comic or otherwise.
We come here to visit Chaplin
and ask for his forgiveness should
we think the world as simple as his

odd little Charlie Chaplin man.
There is no way to get away
from our piddling complexities,
but to fall completely down. Then
who's there to care? We are not saved
even under stone and cedar trees.

Waiting for Recognition

Mid-February
         and we are standing
in the railway station
         of Basel,
waiting to be fetched
         by a stranger host.
Four languages come
         and go and others
I cannot identify.
         Choctaw ghosts
take my arm:
         we want to be recognized
this far from home.
         A native walks as if
she is looking for
         long hair, a feather
dangling down an ear.
         I wait until she
doubles back and asks,
         you aren't him, are you?
My skin shrinks palely
         in the frigid air.

      How to explain
      ashes and my DNA
      scattered way back
      into black Wales
      and Mississippi.
      Even Muskrat
        Coyote
        Crow
    would dodge that one.

Next time we will carry drums,
                    a full pouch
of medicine around
                    our necks for luck
and perseverence.
            These Swiss have an eye
for detail. We might chant,
                    start a small fire.
Or maybe next time have
                    long hair and beads.
She thinks we would like
                    to walk to the place
the reading is to
                    be, saying something
about our lineage
                    and reservations
we do not under-
                    stand Tóntóly clear.
Talking, talking, not
                    stopping, not knowing
the silence of snow,
                    the silence of blood.

Remembering Cap Canaille

So
just
how many
poems do
you have
to write
before 1
from somewhere
like Cassis'
harbor where
a lighthouse
with its low
illumination
green and of
a mysterious
hue comes up
from a depth
beneath your
heart in the
house on the
little cliff
Where Signac
painted pointe
après pointe
Cap Canaille
and the sea,
the changing
light thrown
by gods from
heights that
we can never
know or long
forget, then
an effervescence
of mind only the
one artist perceived in his long regard of sea
and land and light that still in our day holds
the same need to understand all that vanishes from
our life, all that we constantly try to call back?

février 1996
Fondation Camargo

Always Completely at Home

The days we meant to stop in St.-Maximin were
always full of sun and the lure of mountains toward
the north. We never did in all the passing of
the cloister take the time to find the narrow road
up to the door: we were not penitent enough
to drag our indolent bodies through the summer

heat that hung about us in halos of blue flowers
from the Cézanne fields. Perhaps we were a bit afraid
of the spirits that we thought might still linger there
in the dark and gilted skull. Heaviness of monks made
us skirt holy ground and drive round the city square
where old men smoked and played *boules* in the slower hours

of Provençal afternoons. In all that passing,
we never stopped. And now, months past, our minds unfurl
that world: we are driving still in place: the steeple
of St.-Maximin comes in view, and we see swirling
robes of prostitutes and pizza vans and a deep
dust rising from round a game of *boules* that will last

well into the evening hours. Still we drive on through
the broad fields and up the winding road past Pourriéres
as we did before, waving at the old shepherd
with his fall flock near le Puits-d'Auzon, and the bare
summit of Ste.-Victoire glows in the last light poured
from the sun, blessing all the valleys in rose and blue.

In the village that is Vauvenargues, we may atone
with an Amaretto—for we are lovers, wine
if we were not—and contemplate the azure valley
below our table or the château that is vined
with the tangled years of Picasso's art and folly.
He is, locals say, always completely at home.

In Cassis, Early March

The mistral comes down from the north
trailing furies of snow in its wake,
and we close shutters against the dearth
of sun. No one stirs for the sake
of bread or wine. The red tiles quake

and shift in the falling light. The thick
courtyard doors strain in the hard surge
of sound that claims the streets. The quick
wind takes our souls: we sing a dirge
for the slammed boats and the blown birds

and the lost dogs prowling in the dark
of the moon. The lighthouse parts the waves
and trembles in the flow that marks
the stone pier deeper than the days
of chisel and maul. In the deepening haze

we want to pull the walls of the room
closer about us, drink warm tea,
and paint the summer coming soon
to Provence, dream of what should free
us from the wind and calm the sea.

For all that we are sheltered from
keeps pounding in the conch of ears,
the drumming becoming a cadence some
few sojourning souls might fear
the beat of. But now we draw our

sepia days lightly and brush
bare branches with mimosa blooms,
thousands of serins in a rush
of flight, and trace the dying drone
of wind into the sea, its home,

and wait for the change that will come
down from the white harlequin hills
above Vauvenargues. Our walls hum
under the fading sun and sills
are roosts for magpies from those hills.

In Vauvenargues

—Picasso est-il chez lui?
—Ah, oui, complètement.

The proprietor of
Le Restaurant Couscous
swears over his café,
he saw the bald head bob
down the hill and into
the Tabac one dark day

and exit, a carton of
Gaulloises beneath an arm,
or was it Café Crème
Noir? Though it's quite enough
to have just seen the arm,
the head, the rest of him

strolling back up the hill,
pale in the veil of smoke
wrapping around him like
a shroud. The wind was still
as death, he says. His ghost
needed smokes and came back

for more. The mistral did
not blow for weeks, but it
was cold. I kept a cup
of *expresse* tabled outside
in case he needed a hit
to keep his spirits up.

Gwawdodyns for the Fisher King

When I last spoke with you, my old friend,
frost was on the lavender. Low wind
cut our eyes so that one would think the ice
on the streams presaged some bitter end

of an age or race, doomed abstract as
dust. I left San Raphael too fast.
I regret, old friend, my lack of a bold
query. You know I saw the gray ash

upon your face, a mask of torn flesh.
Hindsight tells me I was a fool, flush
with an innocence that has sped me hence
to where I now can say, with no fresh

perspective, you could have made me ask.
Though forbidden words, you could have cast
a runic hand before the hollow doors
that were your eyes, signed me a small cask,

a loaf. But instead, your claws around
the pole, you fished—cursed, cast, reeled, spat, frowned
at the Estérel beyond us—the dream
growing dull as the dent in your crown.

Rue du Faubourg St.-Honoré

1. St.-Philippe du Roule

Head down and reeking of sour sweat, he sits
cross-legged holding in his cupped black hands
a cardboard sign: *j'ai faim*. His one eye flits
back and forth across a soul that you can

never see, nor would even wish to see.
You lay the coins at his feet and leave
with guilt you do not want to show. It's hard
to pass him by when all around guarded

eyes are upon him and you are him, right
to the nth degree: your hands are his, your barred
eyes on the stone, the dream you had last night.

2. Hermès

Behind the windowpane the subtle scarves
present their colors. Every eye that goes
by is flagged and held, the optic nerves
electric with fashion's fine lines frozen

in tableau. The still semaphore competes
with others down the street. Designer boutiques
between Palais de l'Élysée and rue
Royale deny the dream you had, the truth

the beggar will not even tell for fear
of losing face and francs. Gods of ruse
and commerce rule the street. That fact is clear.

3. Résidence du Président

The garden wall begins at the sidewalk
opposite a gallery full of mass
art à la mode. The high wall is chalked
with obsceneties the guards won't let pass

as art. They tell you not to photograph
from either side of the street. They are deaf
to cameras and the traffic at their knees.
The graying wall is ominous: no trees

above the stone. The dream you had last night
is frescoed in the mold above one door, the frieze
so black there's no way you can read it right.

4. Les Chiens

The evidence is everywhere under
your feet, the salt of urine white on gray
cobblestones. The dogs of St.-Honoré
are on the prowl every night. By day

the leash is *très* chic. You allow for crap
at home, but here it's less abstract. The lap
dog really rules the street. Breed depends on
the year. It's the Yorkie now ladies fawn

upon and chauffeurs walk at noon. Next time
you dream eschatological the stone
under your feet will probably turn to lime.

5. Ste.-Marie Madeleine

You turn the Gucci corner onto rue
Royale and see the gray canvas façade
of La Madeleine stark against the hue
of other grays the sky becomes these bad

days. Almost everything you see is fake.
The Gucci in the window is a joke:
the phony leather was made in Itaewon.
Even the deep dream you had last night and

the sweats are suspect: every door you tried
along the street was ivory or horn,
leading you to doubt everything in sight.

6. *Envoi*

God knows rue du Faubourg St.-Honoré
is not real. Laroche, Rykiel, Cartier—
the whole list of shades is not worth the hour
you sat in the Chapelle Expiatoire to pray
and saw snow falling outside on Proust's flowers.

Ballade

from François Villon, Le Testament

Be you seller of papal bulls,
huckster or a shooter of craps,
forger of false coins singeing yourself
like those whose tempers flair,
lying traitors empty of faith,
be you thief, sacker, or looter,
where do you guess the goodies go?
All to the taverns and the girls.

Rhyme, rail, play cymbal, lutes,
like a barefaced lazy jester, joke,
do magic, play flutes, in villages
and cities do farces, cons, moralities,
win at gambling and skittles.
It goes pretty quick—now listen up—
all to the taverns and the girls.

From such rubbish, take a step back.
Plant, mow the fields and meadows,
care for and feed horses and mules
if you're not in the least bit lettered.
If you take it easy you can have it easy,
but if you hack up and scutch hemp,
you don't do you hand over the wages
all to the taverns and the girls?

Your socks, blazing doublets,
gowns, and all your underclothes,
well since you could do worse, take them
all to the taverns and the girls.

I'm talking to you, beer buddies,
sick at soul and big of gut.
You all watch out for this rosy stuff
that turns folks black when they are dead.
Leave it be: it's got a bad bite.
Pass it by the best way you can
and have all due recourse to God,
for a time will come for you to die.

Weather

1. November Clouds

    The clouds are all the same,
heavy with dull wind from Le Havre
    and rain that leaves the stone
streets slow.

    The clouds are not to blame:
a bevy of suicides flies off
    the morning page you read
each day,

    rain or no. Heavy drops
are falling through your life. The clouds
    are here to tell you that
weather

    is not the way to hold
the day. You cannot find the clouds
    answer to anything
but wind.

2. Summer Heat

    It floods up from the underworld
of the Métro and the Seine,
    tunnels flowing full of the dark
summer

    stuff you breathe and are drowning in.
It is thick on the streets
    below Étoile: bright beads of sweat
glimmer

on every face. A mood of June
cannot remove the fear
   from the faces of the mime working
Fouquet's.

   You expect summer heat to change,
even though there is no
   reason to: weather never sends
regrets.

The Poetry Reading near La Californie
after a Day on Golfe Juan

The air is heavy with salt. Someone is making sure nothing will bloom in this room when you are gone. You know outside birds of paradise line the way. You want to be among the flowers a stone or a frog leafed over, camouflaged by a siren of echoing light. Far off, beyond the faces, four walls, and la Californie's lush tropics, mermaids call. You grow gills and swim through a place of sure defeat, your feet fins you never knew you were heir to.

The Judgment of Paris (Whereabouts Unknown)

When you look at Cézanne's apples, you
see that he hasn't really painted apples,
as such.
    —Picasso

With an apple I will astonish Paris.
    —Cézanne

Remember Paris, who herded Priam's flocks,
minding the woolies around Mount Ida's rocks,

Paris, that lonely, lovely, horny son,
exploring wrinkles of Troy's Grand Teton?

His innocence was mostly hidden by
his robe, which bore a rather threadbare fly.

He liked to claim a divine origin
(Cézanne instead gave him a sheepish grin),

longed for Love, and surely would have tried her
among the frolicking ewes on Mount Ida.

When the choice was his, he made it wham! like that—
one was a bit too brainy, the other fat—

selected the juiciest apple, to his eye,
and sent mad Hera storming up on high

and Athena sulking judiciously off
to cure some wanderer of hiccups or the cough.

Aphrodite! O ye gods what a catch!
Shazam! he threw away his robe to match

the goddess' lust in love and to lay claim
to the bobbing apples before his shivering frame.

But, oh alas, soon did he learn the prize
was Menelaos' wife. Down fell the rise

he'd soared on, gone the oats he could've sown.
Poor boy, young as he was, he should've known

you can never trust (with apple) a prude
in the godly state of dishabillitude.

Watching TV at Dooley's, the Early 1950s

for Sundance and June

You would have thought caves and Attic Greek had you been with us: rowed around the walls, we sat like a stone frieze, fallen into a square circle before the silvery appearance. Astonished into our pleasure, we dared not move for fear of losing all of those shadows we leaned into: we hugged slow granite arms unto ourselves, fettered our limbs with silence of chains or caves. What reeled before us we saw as real and saw again: the silver shades we always knew that we were. Somewhere past that light, night rang loud in its stars. The river of sky rushed past our frosted windows. But our eyes swam only farther into that gray and fading screen, its snowy universe of oblivion covering all in a silver light not one soul would ever desire the finis of.

Zen

Whether feather or fin
   looped or lifted high on
      the bright cloud sky where
         all the haze melts away and the sun warms the liquid flight
      the arrow fantails like an
   odd fish homing upstream
to keep an appointment

                              white
with its death and life then breaks downward in a sheer streak of
                              light

to strike the level ground in exultation no poetry can ever know.

Winter's End, 1970

Clouds prophesy: the sky portends
a flood. My mind's a thousand webs
punctured by poetry and trends,
current stuff. Thank God winter ebbs
and dies. The spring semester's gone,
dead as Dante and Calderon.

I'd hoped a literary spring.
Students rebel; the long year ends.
Doting professors fly to Spain.
Picasso's ill. A gardener bends
to pick a pod of paper from
a daisy basket, with aplomb.

My students did not see the truth;
they saw one another and chewed gum.
My fault. And I admit that both
pride and arrogance struck me dumb,
and hot pants and the braless look.
Dactylic hexameter had no luck:

I gave them Homer, heroic deeds.
They preferred travel and communes.
I read them Lucretius, his seeds
of things. I tried to teach them runes,
shadow and substance, and symmetry
from Gilgamesh to Ted Roethke.

I figure up my retirement
and think of moving out of state.
Owls hoot. My head is hard as flint.
Sweating and several days too late,
I check an error, then remind
myself it's glasses or go blind.

All agree spring's a time to move.
My students head for Paris slums.
Picasso's there. So is his love.
They see him everywhere. They run
through more than books to make them wise:
a city of light, laughter, night skies.

Sibyl,

Fate's not a dead leaf
that will rise to any wind:
open up the cave!

We need a guide to lead us
down to twisted roots of things.

Féria de Pâques, Arles 1996

Sitting where Scott and Zelda sat
and their Provençal dog, you lean
into other shadows captured
on the stone tiers of the arena.
The day grays in Arles, sundown
still hours away and the corrida
yet to come. You feel the presence

of known ghosts and hear somewhere at
the back of the wind a low keen,
slow and full of sorrow, buried
under the years of verbena
and lavender. You hear the town
coming to the late corrida
along the one street they will dance

in late tonight after the fat
paella has been eaten and the mean
drunks subdued. No one has hurried
through this day. Still it's more than a
day you see so many of come round
in Provence. The stone corridor
spills its spangled light, the prance

of prelude has begun. The hats
of matadors lifted between
the cheers and salutes, the gloried
Easter afternoon blossoms in a
blaze of mimosa and crimson crowned
with omnipotent gold. Toreadors
bow to Pablo at the wooden fence

and he raises the right hand that
is stained from paint and nicotine.
The faint figure of Françoise, worried
by applause and sand and splintered
against light, rides out. The noise pounds
the sky. You think of Florida
and Key West, Hemingway drunk since

hearing the news of Scott's death,
and of Apollinaire crazy with pain
and throwing out the marks that words
stumbled on. What is the center
of this life if not the sound
of ending? The flow of the corrida
corrupts the sand, and it begins.

The American Heritage Potato

Lying just under potation,
to which it is most assuredly related,
claim the Muscovites,
and somewhat above Potawatomi,
to whom its spiritual qualities are well known,
this edible tuber is even often supposed to be in pot-au-feu,
though the French disclaim it.

In the raw it is
as passive as a dropped fat plum.
It is there for the taking,
incapable of rolling away
because of the nature of its eyes.
No two are alike, unlike the plum,
which is ranked pages above it
and is much sweeter. But you know this,
after having looked up the plural of both:
that both contain an "e" if you go way back.

Vodka has that potatory taste.
So too does Choctaw chock.
I'm talking pomme de terre here
(its fermentation and distillation)
which has made so many of us sing
and just as many dance.
You can call it *potahto* in America if you want,
but not in the company of a Potawatomi
or a Choctaw who has tasted its higher essence.

Postcard to Andrew Grossbardt from the Confluence of the Fourche Maline and Holson Creek, Summerfield, Oklahoma, 1 September 1975

Dear Andy, always the wind is bad as last night's whiskey: keeps your face full of fear you cannot trace to any source. This wind is wild with violets, acorns as large as thundereggs. Here where two rivers meet, odd bones and cracked trees remind you fast the earth will claim its own when the wind and rivers give the word. Even thunder backed by cloud, distant in the somewhere hills, is riding on the wind, and ghosts of a thousand buffalo tumble back into river grass. The way you are drawn to rivers, Andy, is just another mystery you cannot solve. The way that wind wars in your hair or waves can tell you nothing except: you are. Caught three largemouth bass, a blue catfish, and the tent leaks. *Achunanchi!*[*]

---

[*]*Achunanchi:* Choctaw word for "hang in there!"

By the Ruins

for Jerry and Jeanne Easterling

Distance is blue, always, the hue
of smoke is a ghost of centuries
no lookout can ever know past fear.
You count this spot the loneliest
on earth and the best: not one sound,
save trees tell you you are someone
you have to be.

                    The tower's derelict,
but legged enough to lift you over
pines into a wind you haven't felt
for years. The trail you see through haze
hasn't heard hoofbeats since your forbears
fought against the road the trail was then.
The river's dry, its blue a shadow
too thin to trace.

                    You look at hands,
the only map you've ever known
you need. If you could read palms,
these hands would be this blue mountain,
that blue trail, that dry blue river.
To count spent lead and broken flint
you know you need less blue and more
than valleyed flesh and warring bones.

Postcard to David Ray from Poteau Mountain, Runestone State Park

Dear David, I sketched two bears here. I've looked at last pines long enough to know the only scoring they will ever count is the chainsaw screaming down the canyon. Something about the drone of falling trees quicks a shudder in my groin. If I could find that cave, the one I found the long years ago, I would hide the flint I've taken from these doomed hills, after making a fire, then on the smoky walls draw hard bulls or horned men with my Eversharp, and then maybe pray to some dark god hunching in the hills. It's strange, David, alone I always want to sing, with company never. Even a dreamed-up bear or some remembered word or wing will make me dance. Those wilder moments are best I say, but rare as horse feathers nowadays. Sorry: the card can't stand any more of that.

Corniche de l'Estérel

Even now the road is narrow
and curved, the reddish rocks so

close to the pavement that they had
to paint them white. No crosses laid,

but many the dead along this road
between Cannes and San Rafael.

When Scott and Zelda took the villa
and drove into the moon and mood

that linger still on the pages
of Alabama's book, the bridges

were of native stone and curves
red gravel. You had to swerve

dangerously to miss the goats
and potholes. To know the road

you must drive it, leaning into
its slopes and turns, hugging a few

of the rocks so close that you feel
the full force of the Estérel

on your back. Something here wants
to push you in the sea. It's haunted

by spirits of all those who came
this way in search of selves no fame

could satisfy. Drive south, along
the coast at night, but not alone.

Let the moon hang full over the sea,
its mountains almost within reach,

and, if you are lucky, you may know
the Estérel, feel its shadow

move you toward a destiny
never dreamed a possibility.

The Artist as Beachcomber

He walks along the beach where sea and sand
meet, dragging his stick as if to mark there
a joining he wholly approves of, and

takes note of the rose-colored light where
the Estérel juts out to the sea west
of Cannes. He's building castles in the air,

an architecture of the mind he's best
at. Everything he sees becomes canvas
for him to sprawl broad strokes upon, in jest

or high seriousness. He's sculptured busts
of clouds by the time he passes la Croisette.
He stops to doodle in the sand. The last

stroke dissolves into sea. Evening tide lets
loose dog-tongued waves to nudge him toward the hill
where he will take the odd junk from his filet

and place it around the room. Months hence he will
light a blue Gauloise and through a thick veil
of smoke change this day's order of existence.

Picture of Creeley, Rediscovered after Hearing Him Read in Munich, February 1995

Naked Poetry (1st edition)

Sitting there in wrinkled workshirt and jeans
on the edge of the table, right hand
on left knee, left hand closed
by left hip, right foot braced
against the floor, hair and
black background
the same, eyes
straight ahead
and up, one in
shadow
Roman nose
mustache
lips parted
goatee
devil ears
oblivious to
dark raven
and whiskey glass before him

A Book of the Dead

1. the white pages

Coming forth by spring
all recensions sing
of mighty man,
number his right
to lot and land.
No number of odds
will exclude listing
by the gods,
except the heretic,
whose severed self
lies noncommunal, dark.

2. the yellow pages

Coming forth by spring
all recensions bring
a host of slogans
for burial
or for lively dance:
the scale between
the living and the dead
is played again,
and found chords,
A to unlikely Z,
advertise rewards.

3. the cover: rubric

Sunset
and evening star
and one clear call

Winter's End

These sudden ends of time must give us pause.
We fray into the future . . .
   —Richard Wilbur, "Year's End"

Late today the storm clouds come rolling in,
and night is down upon us with a poison
wind. We draw our breaths carefully in, and on
the late winter streets the traffic slows in
obedience to the wind. Children abed
forget their dreams of snow and Christmas sled.

Now is the time their nights are full of flags
atop flowing tents and kites hawking air
rushed from the proverbial northern lair
where the ice folk dance their last jittery jags
before the circuses of southern wind come
to finally drive all glacial gremlins home.

There was a force in winds of yesterday
that we have all but lost. The fateful breeze
for Homer's Greeks brought fame or pregnancies.
In Taos, wind was woman, the Tewas say,
a mean witch of the north and rheumatism.
In Japan, Susanowo sprang from the chasm

of Izanagi's nose: this breath of death
Izanama's spouse sneezed himself free of,
this wind all laden ships ply to lee of,
fleeing the brunt of its immeasurable breadth.
Now the final force of winter's wind wheels
across the roily sky, and thunder peals

like the fiery chariots out of Ezekiel.
Myths such as these indeed do give us cause
to praise first birds headed north. The equinox,
advent of spring, warms us, then makes us feel
heroic: we've fully known our own wrapped worth
in winter's wind, our place in wind on earth.

Fin de Siècle at Schloss Solitude

If you can call it that,
music pounds our heads from
dawn to dark in the schloss
where we wait out the rain,
the snow, the slow coming
of Nordic spring we want
to warm our bodies in.
Karl Eugen's folly squats
on its hill and hosts art
for which the living world
gives not a hoot in hell.

All day dead trimeters
bang up the stairs and quake
our heads toward a madness
we will delight to plan
revenge in. Whoever
is beating knuckles on
the keyboard in the name
of art and missing it
had better watch out for
us. We have had enough
to drive any damned fool

crazy. I take the Swiss
knife from its hiding place
and wet the whetting stone.
I want it sharp, I tell
my poor wife through cotton
in her ears. The long day
is beaten black. Same club.
late she lights a candle
in the echoing hall.
I hold the ready knife
behind my aching back.

Birkenkopf 1998

None of the trees are
older than fifty-odd years:
a lone cross not far

above the town guards the shards
and ashes of lords of war

and Swabians who
died wanting only a few
handfuls of flour to

bake a bread that might undo
what had been done thereunto.

These Flat-Topped Pines Crouch

for W. D. Snodgrass

These flat-topped pines crouch low under heaven.
As I crouch, if I talk, I often cuss
this confounded wood and my own soft heart.
Picasso chose this place and rose at seven
and stood at ease in the mistral like a lush.
J. B. is crawling through the underbrush.

I don't know why I cannot find my house.
It ought to be thicketed somewhere. Fuss
and bother: the stunted trees, the skunk's art
coming on through the dark to then arouse
all one-eyed demons of the mighty bush.
J. B. is crawling through the underbrush.

My name is just as common as a worm,
and not Spanish. If I could converse just
with something inside myself and know it
(have a *tête-à-tête* with some small gentle germ),
I'd make a beeline home. That's where it starts.
I'm circling. I should have been a poet,
but the wood is thick and won't allow old Herm
or the muse to wing it down. I have to rush.
I have to find my house even though it hurts.
J. B. is crawling through the underbrush.

In St.-Maximin-Ste.-Baume with the Old Men at *Boules*, Looking for the Maestro

The old men gather in the late
afternoons in St.-Maximin.
In rose-drenched air the smell of sweat
lingers with just a hint of sin
you cannot quite define. At five
their heavy bodies come alive
with the weight of the *boules* they hold,
and arms are pendulums swung low
in the clicking game. Shadows lull
in doorways, signal time for those
who wager above Mary Magdalene's skull.

Rose fades to lavender: the sun
spills its palette three Cézanne hills
away. And still the game goes on.
The click of clay breaks up the still
voices that seem to hover as though
they were souls reluctant to flow
on the breath of old men. Courtyard
gates start to close. *Tu es en retard,*
someone says across the square while
monks at the cloister bend to prayers
and dust falls on Mary Magdalene's skull.

For hours you sit under plane trees
and watch the old men play, their arms
limp after each smooth cast of the
boules. It never ends. Darkness climbs
the clock tower, then covers the clock.
The slow echo of a song mocks
the time of day in its fervent
joy. Nothing disturbs the old men:

they keep their careful score. The full
moon rises mauve and a low wind
lifts dust on Mary Magdalene's skull.

They all remember him, the way
his ball could make a sweeping curve
and with click and grate ricochet
into position. He had the nerve
to paint his women ugly. Who
knew why? They knew, when he came to
St.-Maximin, his wives in tow,
he'd play as long as they would throw
then offer to buy them wine until
he painted one of them to go
above the bar. Mary Magdalene's skull,

they say, is layered with Jewish gold.
They swear he painted it for fun
the day he beat them all and held
the priestly guard at will within
the walls. He was sketching all askew.
The guard was shocked and finally threw
him out before he finished it.
You see a Death's-head in candlelight
you never stopped to see. To days gone
the old men nod: to theirs, to the night
Picasso painted Mary Magdalene.

The players case the *boules* and, contrite,
cross the square and cross themselves. Light
from the moon pales them into ghosts as lean
as lavender in the bluing night
kneeling above Mary Magdalene.

Deputy Finds Dean's Tombstone on Highway

—St.Louis Post-Dispatch, 18 July 1998

Over forty years ago, I saw you
in my mirror mornings before the slow
days dawned. Working the hoot-owl shift miles
above Bohemia and in love with smiles
anyone gave, I was you to the core,
looked like you even then. Hung my hands in
pockets lightly exactly the way you did,
and wore the light blue pants.

                    Our names the same
signaled something I tried my best to grasp.
Maybe I have it now. But for you, Jimmy,
I would have remained in the north country
and never have known the freedom of road
and will. I was a slow rebel, double
for you in the smoky taverns of Oregon
where lost women and mournful men spilled their
lives on Saturday nights.

                  You taught me how
to desire and what the desiring is for:
departure. The setting out must go on
and on. So I think of this these decades
late after reading the Reuters release.
In July there are shivers in Fairmount.
Someone's life somewhere is about to change,
the tailgate down and the bed empty and scarred.
Your name, our name, Jimbo, flat on the road
sliding west with traffic: that's the way it
ought to always be this far from Eden
or South Bend.

This far from the lumbering
towns or lots full of OICs, I see you
still, the standing shadow in every ditch
or curve someone sometime did not make
in a momentary reach for misguided
glory. The pickup reaches home toward
midnight. The two men, in late middle age,
lean their arms on the rim of the empty bed
and gaze into the nothing they have carried
to the sanctuary of the deep Indiana fields.

Epitaph for J(ohn). B(erryman).

He did his bit
for American lit:
he wrote in fits,
then called it quits.

Monsieur le Marquis de Vauvenargues

He never liked it much
in winter. The wind ripped
through the heather with such

blue force and through the cracks
it made shudders rattle
and unlocked doors fly back.

Too cold to concentrate,
to paint, he said and returned
to La Californie late

in the rosy autumn
and then over the hill
to the farm, Notre-Dame-

de-Vie. The slip still flowed
in his veins. The Maestro spun
the potter's wheel, bowed

under the St.-Claude he
himself made out of clay.
Not a good place to be,

he said, the house under
Ste.-Victoire. Summers were
also fierce, with thunder.

It had reminded him
of catacombs, the cold
stone depths. The awful dim-

ness of all the ancient rooms
clouded his vision. He'd
always dreaded the gloom

which often had infused
his luck in high Provence.
On the Côte d'Azur he mused

on final years and fine
pots fired with horns or hats
or faces. Most of the time

he mused, refused to stop
ceramic toil, prints by
the hundreds, a whole crop

of sketches in his eighth
decade of taking chances.
The Maestro kept the faith:

everything grew in
great abundance. Even
the oils began again,

before he died the un-
eventful death he said
would be a shipwreck none

ever could survive.
The last wife, her face in
pieces on the chair, gave

orders, and it was done:
the long road back in wind
and snow, and the lot gone

bad in cruel April,
and Pablo laid in that
stony courtyard while

a hard rain came down.
Singly or two by two
the mourners stood around

the gate, only to be
sent away without hope
of entry. The house, free

now of clatter or calm,
was too upset for guests
to come. Paloma and Claude,

the other son, an old
friend from Madrid, scribes,
Monsieur le Maire, were told

to go away. The château
turned even the mistral
from its cold track to blow

another way. Like the ark
on Ararat, Monsieur
le Marquis de Vauvenargues

lay as flat as he must,
of necessity, among shards
of time he could never trust.

The Marsh Bird

Not by wisdom do poets write.
  —Plato

This slow bird
counts his years by density
of mud.

His odd boot
of a bill is just as much
a foot

as not;
to see him walk you'd think
him out

of place
with his yardy legs half-stuck
and weedy face.

Strange thing:
this slow bird must be mad and mired
to sing.

The Cave on Cavanal Mountain

The highest hill in the world, 1999 feet.
—Oklahoma signpost

The wind tells you by its blue moan
across the cave's dark mouth
at dawn

how it is to be above the ground.
The glyphs inside the cave
step around

the walls like hunters stalking buffalo.
The only direction
you know

to go is after the thrown spear,
the sickled moon, the masked air,
the running deer.

The puzzle that you read always reads
the same: the hunt is cracking stone
and needs.

The pointed chase runs always into dark:
the beast leaps into itself, the downed man
forgets to bark.

Portrait in Seven Parts with Nightscape

i.

Yellow hair,
a leaning nose,
stars on the chin,
no clouds.

ii.

Background not
woods: Ste.-Victoire
through open
casement,
sky,
water,
words: *Le musée est en Paris.*

iii.

The way uphill unmarked,
a well with no rope,
a goat
with one eye
on its back.

iv.

Picasso's dogs
guessing
out loud.

v.

A cuckoo clock
crowing
at the moon
geometrically.

vi.

A fast goodnight
on crooked stairs.

vii.

The moon entering
the open window,
shoving piled shadows
aside, sitting on
the chair, watching
the sleeper dream.

Heading East Out of Rock Springs

for Andrew Grossbardt, long gone

On a high plateau where the earth rounds off
the edge of nothing and the sky pours down
like hail so heavy that the pickup squats
on its springs and groans toward the horizon,
you think of Andy, all those years long gone.

What had he thought when he left Missoula
and headed toward a millennium of doubt
he called poetry?—his own old Ford fooling
itself under the hood and gasping out
of the long valleys, then turning south

onto the plains. Then those years of Missouri,
camped on a side street in Kirksville, among
the detritus of sojourners, the misery
of travelers haunting him like a song
and something solid growing daily wrong

inside his head. You remember Andy's hands
if you remember right: the way they shook
like aspen leaves, always in flux and
pale. Past Red Desert you begin to look
for signs that mean trails end or roads fork.

The land grows abstract as your horoscope.
What you read once as bright now reads dim
in the falling light. His fine-boned poems lope
like deer on the living language plains and seem
to fade to haze, and are all that's left of him.

Sundown. An owl heads for Cheyenne. The pickup
drones toward the dark. You hardly knew the hills
then, though you recognized the thirst and the cup
and watched him drink at the roiling source until
he knew the strength of word and the word could kill.

Between Boot Hill and the shopping mall, you park
the truck under hanging light. The road's been long
and there's long to come, Andy. You can't face dark
turns to Dis or Denver without sleep: no song
worth the risk nor the risk worth this time going.

Birkenkopf 2000

Two years later and the trees are down,
swept flat by wind propelled from the west
with the weight of ten thousand crashing
Messerschmidts. The storm laid waste
the forest that covered remnants of war.

Nor did the woods beyond the mount
of ash escape the wind that bore
the century toward its wild end: trees
a hundred years green and even more
uprooted, testament to natural war

nothing is sacred to: *Cuernica*
in larch and fir, mother earth slammed
into upheaval, roots in air,
cross-timbered roads, streams dammed,
and all Baden-Wurttemberg maimed

by a force nothing could reckon with.
Now mid-February with its short
memory forces buds through broken
limbs, and the crows again hold forth,
wings brilliant in the raucous court.

Giuseppe's Song for His Annelise

—Commissioned at La Piazetta, Stuttgart, Germany, 23.02.00

All the roses, all the heather
North of Napoli I gather

Now into this song for my love,
Elegant Annelise. My love,

Lovely as roses, pale heather
In rain or sun or all weather,

Shines with radiance from above,
Elegant Annelise, my love.

The Fox at Agay

From the hedge by the side of the road
with a leap and a bound for the other side,
a fox breaks for the hill and the broad
cover of green. We brake, and the night
shudders, stops. A gray flash, a burst
of darker light than ours: the fox
has his tail in level tow, the first

wild thing we have seen in the south
of France, except of course the birds.
We begin to half-believe tales how
the paysans stayed alive. We heard
they nearly starved during the War.
Some had eaten anything that moved
or what they could snare by haywire

or rope or kill by stone. This one
was grandson of grandsons who some way
survived in the high mountain caves
and woods, and he would not succumb
to a mere glare of the lights he saw
as moons moving along the road
in Agay. A moment as short as the caw

of a crow and he was gone, his muscled
tail sliding through the moonlit shrubs
and the flat-topped pines of the Estérel.
We felt little more than the rub
of his crossing, but it was enough
to remind us that something had come
back to our lives we once had loved.

Visiting Picasso

Just north from Pourrières the winding road
skirts wide fields where the Romans fought the horde
of Ambrons. A hundred thousand rotted
in this valley, and south the Arc ran red.

Crossing terraces built from bones, we praise
the rich ground, drive up Pain de Munition
where Caius Marius lay in wait, the crazed
tribes on a run for Rome with no notion

the Legions were men enough to stop them.
After battle, shipwreck, old age, that's all:
only debris is left. Picasso's death then

would be a shipwreck, he said and left no will.
He wanted no survivors. Those lucky to swim
the straits would find no lighthouse on the hill.

e๐

The road up is treacherous and narrow.
A slip of wheel and you join the later dead,
Maquisard buried at odd places and just so
to warn others. At le Puits-de-Rian, we head

west to Vauvenargues and take the going slow.
On a long spring Sunday the sky is lead,
the same kind of day she took Picasso
down this same road through April snow. Cars slid

off the track and on again. Headlights blurred
into a coming fog that would not clear.
The Maestro's ship had sunk. Jacqueline's word

was now law: burial at the château, near
the front door. We park and watch a lone bird
circle the Maestro's house, then disappear.

La Vieille Madame à la Machine à Sous

Saturday night in Bandol and the mistral
bends the palms with an unrelenting flow
that will not cease until the night grows
empty and the lights are finally dimmed. Now all

the women in their snug furs have returned
to play *les machines à sous*. You hear them
insert the coins and see the flash of dream
glaze their eyes. The steady mistral churns

the sea, and waves roll up the deserted pier.
The moon is full in its slot of sky, and clouds
that pass are tokens of what could or could
not be. An old madame sees it as clear

as any sign she's ever seen. She chooses
the Triple Wild and has the pit boss bring
her francs, a bucket full. She twists her ring
for added luck. A man *en face* loses

to a 5 x 5 and curses in Provençal.
He heads for the door still calling it bad names.
The old madame flips her fingers the same
way at everything she dismisses: *trop mal*.

She's here to win and doesn't care who knows
it. She slams the handle down, and coins drop
out as if they do not know how to stop.
The mistral is her friend she says. It goes

with her, down from the hungry hills above
to the edge of the broad deep sea. There were days,
she says, we had neither *sous* nor sow to pay
for bread, but we could live on country love

and good red wine. She pulls and Wilds appear:
it's a jackpot: the coins pile into the tray
and spill onto the floor. Outside the waves
pound the pier, and the sky begins to clear.

Rubaiyat for a Pair of Heroes

from the photographs by David Douglas Duncan

Coop brought the Maestro a white ten-gallon hat
and shiny six-shooter from Hollywood that
neither could hit the broad side of a can
of paint with. Doves left the loft, the fat cat

next door fled the vicinity, the dogs ran
behind the god-awful goat. Tree bark and sand
flew until the fast draws failed and the shells
gave out. The heroes hitched up their baggy pants

and lurched back inside to have a large Vittel,
four fingers each, then another round, to hell
with all them galoots who wouldn't shoot it out
fair and square. Pablo tipped his hat to tell

Jacqueline the villa was safe from the banditos
in the big paint can. Coop drawled around Picasso's
studio. Sit, the Maestro said, and Coop wound
his legs round a chair reserved for mementos

no one dared touch except a partner bound
for glory out on the range. What they found
in common was the unadorned in art that
lasted: both had their feet on solid ground.

On the Hill Back of La Ciotat

Poppies begin to bloom among
the wild rosemary and lavender:
the red swath starts meandering
toward the sea. Olive trees belong

here where the wind twists the fruit firm
and trunks into such grotesque form
no normal axe will ever fell them.
We take the drive up slowly, turn

with caution on the narrow roads
whose walls are mostly fallen down
and even more down than we can
say since the hill is steep and broad.

Far down we see a house someone
called a home, or rather we see
more fallen stone the sea will claim.
Once a home but now a ruin upon

the hill few seldom climb. Poppies
lean against its remaining walls
as if to stall the last stones'
completely falling down. I will

remember to count my last days
by rock and flower: to end as smooth
as loose stone in a flow of poppies,
ah, what brilliance and what praise!

Ithaka 2001

Hope all your Ithakas are good ones.
    —Cavafy

Seems ages on the hill above the rocky point
I have kept my eyes on the horizon where sky
drops to sea. No sign of any ship I do not
recognize, just the ragtag worn-out fishing fleet
about to sink. No single sail grabbing the wind
and fifty men at oars to tell us you are back.
This is no Ithaka now you would own up to,
your old wife mad, your queer son gone, your dog
years dead. The old men gathered here like the food
and wine, but do not give a hoot about the place.
You might as well have gone down in the fishy sea:

this is no Ithaka you would want to rule. Still we
hope for your long return, the foolish old friends of
the foolish king who went away to war for fear
of losing what we have lost anyway, although
you, somewhere landbound or adrift on the deep, still
may dream of coming back to stony Ithaka,
to a faithful wife and infant son. Wherever
you are, I send you these heavy words on a wind
that has treated us all badly: there is little
use for you to come back home old and mortified.
Ithaka is not the Ithaka it was. For god's

sake, be strong. We have grown even older hoping.
Perhaps you have found another Ithaka elsewhere
in the wide world, a soft and welcome country that
nourishes you in a way we never can again.
I wish you well, but I must keep on hoping that
you will come back again. You could teach us a way
at least to cope with the thing that has befallen
us. The tourists' shops and the garish touring boats

prosper, but they are in the hands of foreigners.
The breeding cattle prized by Philoitius the bankers
in Pylos hold for the debts Penelope incurred.

The suitors had no staying power when the booze
ran out. No one manned the presses nor tended vines.
Pirates from Samos got the last of goats and sheep
when we tried to take the herds across to Argive
lands. Hardly any of us are left who give a damn
about the state. I am here every day, though hope
runs thin. I know you will return sometime. It is
no Ithaka to brag about. Hope you will bring
our salvation in some form. Yellow gold would help
and medicine that would somehow cure all the pain
of mind and body. We are ill in Ithaka.

Lay

from François Villon, Le Testament

Death, I object to your rigor
which has taken my mistress away
and still you are not satisfied
if you can't see me wasting away.
Since then, I have had no strength, no vigor.
But alive how did she harm you,
Death?

We two were one and had one heart.
If it is dead, strength is thus gone.
Oh yes, or else I'm living dead,
as images do, in the heart,
Death.

The First Féria of the Third Millennium, Arles Easter Monday

At the barrera Anthony Quinn jeers Monsieur
le Président. The boy from Arles should have
at least one ear, so sure he was with the kill.
The crowd waves white scarfs, claps in unison,
until the ear is granted and the matador
bows. Pablo, just above the judges, leans
slightly forward, nods to the protege
of an old comrade who once killed six bulls *seul*
on a hot Pâques afternoon. But Pablo is dead
these many years, and Tony much too old
to give a damn and sit through wind and rain
and cold to see six bulls die and no one

gored. Yet the boy from Arles with his hour
on the home sand and two good bulls was brave
enough to summon spirits of those whose will
defined their art. Fitzgerald catches the sun
for a moment with his little dog, much more
at ease here than in Antibes. Zelda finds
the image and snaps the shutter on the way
they were. The crowd rises and shakes the cruel
rain off its hide, wants only now to be fed
the tubs of paella steaming on the mall.
The arena grows empty. Figures in the rain
hold their shape, then slowly dissolve on stone,

ghosts that refuse to leave this place where
the same thing goes on forever, waves
of time repeating waves. What was here still
is here. Image never fully fades. One
photo taken eighty years ago, more
or less, evokes a clear sense of the time
Scott and Zelda invented lives in a way

that holds the elegance and grace of style.
Between bull and matador there is no dread
of the act of finality. So too the fall
of fictive lives. Having guts to remain
steadfast is no sin you have to atone

for: Hemingway called it grace under pressure.
César Rincon faced six bulls years ago, gave
Arles an opening day they will recall until
the last posters blur. Pablo would have done
the corrida on copper plates before
the moon went down behind the marshy rim
of the Camargue. Today was such a day
as that, and the evocation just as real.
The boy from Arles was steadfast in his need,
from the smooth work of cape to the grace of kill.
The flowing day repeats itself in your mind
and what you think is past is never gone.

In Aix-en-Provence

There were *canards*
with yellow feet
and *saucisses noirs*
ready to eat

hanging primely
by window pane
in the boucherie
on rue Cézanne

when we were lost
and looking for
the short road east
to Vauvenargues.

The crazy streets
we tried to go
all came to meet
cours Mirabeau.

We found a place
to lunch just so:
on duck, a glass
of wine, a loaf

of Provence bread.
Picasso sat
above our heads,
Lump and Yan at

his kneading hands,
and next to them,
guess if you can—
thumbtacked and trimmed

(you know it well),
the horny sneer
straight out of hell—
what king was there.

The Poet's Paradise

I have put the manuscript in the mail,
my dear, & now again the wait begins.
How can I tell you of the awesome ends
I've tried to make means meet & stay hail

and hearty to boot? With both tooth & nail
I've ladled away the deadly gush that lends
itself to lines I get emotional in.
Blood rises at the thought: again I'll fail.

Something of myself I have torn away.
Hope, my dear, is exorcism of cliché.
What matters now is fear & the one right word:

wind, rain, hail, night, day.
The poet's paradise is no delay
of mail, his lady's love, & the one right word.

Agamemnon

i. *Watchman, what of the night?*

The long toil of night
has made me old.
There is no light,
only the cold
fires of heaven
dim and distant . . .

Watchman, what of the night?

The winds come, the winds go,
waves break upon the shore
cold and senseless.
There is no light
and old men die.

ii. *Homecoming*

What is that stain
upon the stone?
How changed this shore
since those green years.
Let us fret no more
and put away our fears:
dismiss the guard.
We are grown old.

Come, let us bathe away our toil
and give praise for Argive soil.
The long chain has turned to rust.
No need for public declaration:
our house shall rest on trust.

Whose shadow is that among our men?
Why do they turn?
Is this a portion of the dream?

iii. *On the Argive Plain*

Over there, over there beyond
that line of sun-drenched stone
lies Agamemnon dead somewhere
about the ruins.

The bronze shield, stark and real,
overhead blazes indifference
on this land where man
gave way to man.

As sure as existence that man
lived, died, and was mourned,
is mourned. What matters proof?
The need is only the knowing.

Listen: you too can hear the clash
of sword on bone, the falling stone,
the confusion of the Argives,
the woman's awesome excuses,
the wild rhythm of the Erinyes,
the silence of the gods . . .

Stark and real, the bronze shield
rolls on. We cannot atone,
cannot condone,
and Kassandra's words are wild as ever.

The Snow Bird

His flight across the white waste
disturbs no one and no thing:
he touches softly down on the sterile field
like a carrier of some clean disease
delivering an augur random notes:
the song is all but silent to all ears,
the dance a pattern only snows and old men know.
He will stay, this quiet bird, only so long
as he has need to search for sustenance
among mirrored crystals of this white sea,
then rise, finally rise, on silver wings
into the feathered air, his final bed.

Twister

The far woods turn dark as soot of chimneys;
a solid tunnel of sky siphons
up the soul of the farm,
then takes the farm.

The far mother, a choir of orphans in her ears,
moans through straw pointed into her throat;
hail cracks against the ground
like thunder eggs.

The far neighbor rushes naked and hard
down some sudden creek, the taste of
doom cold on his lost lips;
finally, the rain,

falling, falling, and the faint odor of lilacs
you know not where.

Ikaros 1940

Days you fell
into leaves
and wrapped
a crazy wing
into your skin
and bones, hawks
were diving
into kites.

The moon threw
off rings fast
as usual
lovers clothes.

Foxes forgot
their noses
and joined
the circus
of the trees.

The world
was crazy
with the wind
you knew you
could catch
from the razored
mountain peak.

So you fell
from light
through light,
your gypsy
wings raining
toward the sun,
and hit the
slanting ground
behind the barn
with a gunning
buzzard's run,
the sky's last
condor coming
home to roost.

Owl

His question marks evenings
when hills hardly hold
dead day's last light.

Night stops his dreamer's *who*.
Woods, river, knoll,
and field are right

for answer and killer wing.
Blind as bats and fear,
the owl is all ear.

Sound is his sustenance:
ears sharp as a sickled moon,
talons loud to crack crazed bone.

Listen: the owl is silent
across the night, gone
to split skulls on wood or stone.

Rondeau for a Shovelbill Catfish, at the Buffalo Hole, Fourche Maline River, à la Research du Temps Perdu, January 2003

On the bottom of the buffalo hole
lurks a shovelbill cat, a slow
mole scooping through the heavy loam,
his eyes near blind from the deep home
and quotidian quest and toll.

He counts his world a world below
all other fish. His need is to go
profoundly into the froth and foam
on the bottom

and ram his flat jaws into and hold
the fertile pasture of his old
earth and graze on mussels and worms.
He knows hook and line and the warm
smell of bait, dough balls—and death, cold
on the bottom.

Picasso never caught those bones
on a dirty plate, nor were there tomes
nor even a tune written by court
poets way back then when they ought.
That mug would frighten the worst of gnomes
at bridges, snakes on the bottom.

Magpie

Pitch black and white and lively all over,
his hide is far from what you often call crow.

He'll steal you blind behind your back or trade
you dead skunk's eyes for a coin or plastic rose.

To check his thorny den you'd think him rat
right at home among his foul and foreign cheese.

You'll never catch him mousing in the grass;
he'd rather take your dirty socks and gos-

sip through his nose a higher sort of sass.
Odd bird, he speaks plainest with a forked tongue.

West of Cassis

Loving the sand and water the way you knew you always would,
        you swear you will find a niche to keep you close to the
        broken shore, where the fishy sea accepts
        the white *calanques* below the Laestragonian cliffs
        under the noonday sun.

Finding driftwood ground smooth as glass and sand dollars
        with their intricate leaves
makes you forget that other land and the inky inland clouds
        where the sky was lead and ranchers were driven mad
        by the ghosts of wolves.

Here the shore is always backed by lavender and the sea a wine no
        dumb sailor could deny.
The stormy plains will never again roar at your back *come home,*
        come home,
not while you face the sun and another kind of wind and the world
        fans out beyond you like a flag.

West of Cassis, where rivers end and the *Mediterranée* bends her
        current hard to the tall north,
you find yourself leaning still the way water wants toward a solid
        acceptance of debris:
whatever flows past will ebb and you must hold the in-between: the eel-
        infested rush, the graved and tumbled stone, the slushed
        peelings and parings called love, the poetry
        you live by.

Taos as Purgatory

A little guts, self drama and it's done.
—Richard Hugo

Masked Kachina dolls gauge our sins
and Tewas take our coins
for the dance they say
will make our lives
like spring.

The heated pool at our last lodge
at high noon seems odd as hot
green chili we know
at last we have
to try.

The plaza is a blaze of conchas
and sun-drugged freaks burnt black
by wind and stares.
Two Hopis hunker
under

blankets and inquisitorial rage.
The sun drops heavy as doom.
The adobe night
and sirens wail
had dreams.

Morning ascent into Sangre de Cristo:
a deliverance cooled by pines
and icy streams.
The earth uncracks
and suddenly
we smile.

Epithalamion: Villanelle for September 7, 2002

for Blake and Melissa

All the flowers are wrapped in the blessing sun,
and with this union of two best friends today
something as lasting as this light has begun

to wreathe the bride and groom. Nothing's undone:
hands are joined. All the faces calm with tears say
all the flowers are wrapped in the blessing sun;

so let this joining last, not be undone
by storm or cloud, for this day is yours. This day
something as lasting as the light has begun,

a bright moment to shape two lives as one
for all time to come and for all the ways
all the flowers are wrapped in the blessing sun.

As flowers climb a trellis and runners run
a lattice work, your joined lives will display
something lasting that light has begun,

something lasting as long as there is sun.
With sons and daughter near, praise the day:
you are the flowers wrapped in the blessing sun,
light lasting as something on this day begun.

In Memory of Dora Maar

When the mistral swept the *allées* clean
and slammed the country courtyard gates
and Ste.-Victoire was cracked by keen
and wore a shroud on its north face,

she haunted him. We saw her ghost
mostly through Pablo's eyes, where not
everything was focused right. A lost
mongrel he thought she was, in a rut

she couldn't claw out of for the sake
of art or love. Picasso thought
she'd fade right in with Paris fakes
and her art slow down, but she thought

otherwise and painted another view
of herself, a weeping woman
Picasso couldn't face, and through
the mad years grew madder still than

the others he had ruined by love
or use. She followed him so far
south she forgot her life, then lunged
on past her former love and art,

past madness, into a mood so maud-
lin it wore her down. A recluse sworn
to outlasting his other loves, she sold
her work only to live and mourn.

Elegy for the Old Man beside the Road to Nans les Pins

It whispers in his ears,
      the wind caressed by sun,
        gently.

He hears his body's hollows
      echoing from skull to rib cage,
        softly.

He does not yearn
      to lie under the flat-topped pines
        again

or mingle among old vining friends
      who arm and shoulder knew him
        always.

He wishes now only to hear
      what the low wind
        wafts

across the ripening fields:
      all the things he has been
        yesterdays.

Villa Serbelloni Revisited, February 2003

for Caroline de la Tour du Pin and Gianna Celli

Twelve years since the bells of Bellagio
have rung for us, and now we hear
them tolling for a return in snow
we find a little hard to bear,
for then it was a time below
the daylight now. The month was clear
with springing mountains, with flowers
in the Melzi gardens, with showers

greening the lawns flowing down to
the lapping lake edge. Our first cry
is for that time ago that threw
us headlong into poetry,
the rush of images into
the sound and sense that we tried
to give to our lost lives. We raise
our eyes to the hill, the olives,

the haze, the orchard silver in
the morning light. High up the hill
sunlight strikes stone and begins
to wake the Frati and the villa
from their ochre sleep. The high thin
Sunday brings its time ago still
into the snow that is Bellagio
without regret, and what we know

begins to flow back warm as summer
rain was then below these mountains
that were topped with clouds no thunder
could disperse. Memories remain
of old Bellagio, and murmurs
of spring beneath the snow begin
to wake us to this paradise,
to more than we could then surmise.

JIM BARNES is an internationally recognized poet and translator. He has received two Rockefeller Foundation Bellagio Residency Fellowships, two Camargo Foundation Fellowships, and a Senior Fullbright Fellowship to Switzerland. His 1992 book of poetry, *The Sawdust War,* won the Oklahoma Book Award in Poetry. His other poetry volumes include *Paris, On a Wing of the Sun, The Fish on Poteau Mountain, The American Book of the Dead, A Season of Loss,* and *La Plata Cantata.* He is also author of the American Book Award–winning autobiography *On Native Ground: Memoirs and Impressions.*

Illinois Poetry Series
Laurence Lieberman, Editor

History Is Your Own Heartbeat
Michael S. Harper (1971)

The Foreclosure
Richard Emil Braun (1972)

The Scrawny Sonnets and Other
    Narratives
Robert Bagg (1973)

The Creation Frame
Phyllis Thompson (1973)

To All Appearances: Poems New
    and Selected
Josephine Miles (1974)

The Black Hawk Songs
Michael Borich (1975)

Nightmare Begins Responsibility
Michael S. Harper (1975)

The Wichita Poems
Michael Van Walleghen (1975)

Images of Kin: New and Selected
    Poems
Michael S. Harper (1977)

Poems of the Two Worlds
Frederick Morgan (1977)

Cumberland Station
Dave Smith (1977)

Tracking
Virginia R. Terris (1977)

Riversongs
Michael Anania (1978)

On Earth as It Is
Dan Masterson (1978)

Coming to Terms
Josephine Miles (1979)

Death Mother and Other Poems
Frederick Morgan (1979)

Goshawk, Antelope
Dave Smith (1979)

Local Men
James Whitehead (1979)

Searching the Drowned Man
Sydney Lea (1980)

With Akhmatova at the Black Gates
Stephen Berg (1981)

Dream Flights
Dave Smith (1981)

More Trouble with the Obvious
Michael Van Walleghen (1981)

The American Book of the Dead
Jim Barnes (1982)

The Floating Candles
Sydney Lea (1982)

Northbook
Frederick Morgan (1982)

Collected Poems, 1930–83
Josephine Miles (1983; reissue, 1999)

The River Painter
Emily Grosholz (1984)

Healing Song for the Inner Ear
Michael S. Harper (1984)

The Passion of the Right-Angled
    Man
T. R. Hummer (1984)

Dear John, Dear Coltrane
Michael S. Harper (1985)

Poems from the Sangamon
John Knoepfle (1985)

In It
Stephen Berg (1986)

The Ghosts of Who We Were
Phyllis Thompson (1986)

Moon in a Mason Jar
Robert Wrigley (1986)

Lower-Class Heresy
T. R. Hummer (1987)

Poems: New and Selected
Frederick Morgan (1987)

Furnace Harbor: A Rhapsody of the
    North Country
Philip D. Church (1988)

Bad Girl, with Hawk
Nance Van Winckel (1988)

Blue Tango
Michael Van Walleghen (1989)

Eden
Dennis Schmitz (1989)

Waiting for Poppa at the Smithtown
    Diner
Peter Serchuk (1990)

Great Blue
Brendan Galvin (1990)

What My Father Believed
Robert Wrigley (1991)

Something Grazes Our Hair
S. J. Marks (1991)

Walking the Blind Dog
G. E. Murray (1992)

The Sawdust War
Jim Barnes (1992)

The God of Indeterminacy
Sandra McPherson (1993)

Off-Season at the Edge of the World
Debora Greger (1994)

Counting the Black Angels
Len Roberts (1994)

Oblivion
Stephen Berg (1995)

To Us, All Flowers Are Roses
Lorna Goodison (1995)

Honorable Amendments
Michael S. Harper (1995)

Points of Departure
Miller Williams (1995)

Dance Script with Electric Ballerina
Alice Fulton (reissue, 1996)

To the Bone: New and Selected
    Poems
Sydney Lea (1996)

Floating on Solitude
Dave Smith (3-volume reissue,
    1996)

Bruised Paradise
Kevin Stein (1996)

Walt Whitman Bathing
David Wagoner (1996)

Rough Cut
Thomas Swiss (1997)

Paris
Jim Barnes (1997)

The Ways We Touch
Miller Williams (1997)

The Rooster Mask
Henry Hart (1998)

The Trouble-Making Finch
Len Roberts (1998)

Grazing
Ira Sadoff (1998)

Turn Thanks
Lorna Goodison (1999)

Traveling Light:
Collected and New Poems
David Wagoner (1999)

Some Jazz a While:
Collected Poems
Miller Williams (1999)

The Iron City
John Bensko (2000)

Songlines in Michaeltree: New and
    Collected Poems
Michael S. Harper (2000)

Pursuit of a Wound
Sydney Lea (2000)

The Pebble: Old and New Poems
Mairi MacInnes (2000)

Chance Ransom
Kevin Stein (2000)

House of Poured-Out Waters
Jane Mead (2001)

The Silent Singer: New and Selected
    Poems
Len Roberts (2001)

The Salt Hour
J. P. White (2001)

Guide to the Blue Tongue
Virgil Suárez (2002)

The House of Song
David Wagoner (2002)

X =
Stephen Berg (2002)

Arts of a Cold Sun
G. E. Murray (2003)

Barter
Ira Sadoff (2003)

The Hollow Log Lounge
R. T. Smith (2003)

In the Black Window: New and
    Selected Poems
Michael Van Walleghen (2004)

A Deed to the Light
Jeanne Murray Walker (2004)

Controlling the Silver
Lorna Goodison (2005)

Good Morning and Good Night
David Wagoner (2005)

American Ghost Roses
Kevin Stein (2005)

Battles and Lullabies
Richard Michelson (2005)

The Disappearing Trick
Len Roberts (2006)

Eroding Witness
Nathaniel Mackey (1985)
Selected by Michael S. Harper

Palladium
Alice Fulton (1986)
Selected by Mark Strand

Cities in Motion
Sylvia Moss (1987)
Selected by Derek Walcott

The Hand of God and a Few Bright
 Flowers
William Olsen (1988)
Selected by David Wagoner

The Great Bird of Love
Paul Zimmer (1989)
Selected by William Stafford

Stubborn
Roland Flint (1990)
Selected by Dave Smith

The Surface
Laura Mullen (1991)
Selected by C. K. Williams

The Dig
Lynn Emanuel (1992)
Selected by Gerald Stern

My Alexandria
Mark Doty (1993)
Selected by Philip Levine

The High Road to Taos
Martin Edmunds (1994)
Selected by Donald Hall

Theater of Animals
Samn Stockwell (1995)
Selected by Louise Glück

The Broken World
Marcus Cafagña (1996)
Selected by Yusef Komunyakaa

Nine Skies
A. V. Christie (1997)
Selected by Sandra McPherson

Lost Wax
Heather Ramsdell (1998)
Selected by James Tate

So Often the Pitcher Goes to Water
 until It Breaks
Rigoberto González (1999)
Selected by Ai

Renunciation
Corey Marks (2000)
Selected by Philip Levine

Manderley
Rebecca Wolff (2001)
Selected by Robert Pinsky

Theory of Devolution
David Groff (2002)
Selected by Mark Doty

Rhythm and Booze
Julie Kane (2003)
Selected by Maxine Kumin

Shiva's Drum
Stephen Cramer (2004)
Selected by Grace Schulman

The Welcome
David Friedman (2005)
Selected by Stephen Dunn

Michelangelo's Seizure
Steve Gehrke (2006)
Selected by T. R. Hummer

Other Poetry Volumes

Local Men and *Domains*
James Whitehead (1987)

Her Soul beneath the Bone:
Women's Poetry on Breast Cancer
Edited by Leatrice Lifshitz (1988)

Days from a Dream Almanac
Dennis Tedlock (1990)

Working Classics: Poems on
Industrial Life
*Edited by Peter Oresick and Nicholas
Coles* (1990)

Hummers, Knucklers, and Slow
Curves: Contemporary Baseball
Poems
Edited by Don Johnson (1991)

The Double Reckoning of
Christopher Columbus
Barbara Helfgott Hyett (1992)

Selected Poems
Jean Garrigue (1992)

New and Selected Poems, 1962–92
Laurence Lieberman (1993)

The Dig and *Hotel Fiesta*
Lynn Emanuel (1994)

For a Living: The Poetry of Work
*Edited by Nicholas Coles and Peter
Oresick* (1995)

The Tracks We Leave: Poems on
Endangered Wildlife of North
America
Barbara Helfgott Hyett (1996)

Peasants Wake for Fellini's *Casanova*
and Other Poems
*Andrea Zanzotto; edited and
translated by John P. Welle and
Ruth Feldman; drawings by
Federico Fellini and Augusto Murer*
(1997)

Moon in a Mason Jar and *What My
Father Believed*
Robert Wrigley (1997)

The Wild Card: Selected Poems,
Early and Late
*Karl Shapiro; edited by Stanley
Kunitz and David Ignatow* (1998)

Turtle, Swan and *Bethlehem in Broad
Daylight*
Mark Doty (2000)

Illinois Voices: An Anthology of
Twentieth-Century Poetry
*Edited by Kevin Stein and G. E.
Murray* (2001)

On a Wing of the Sun
Jim Barnes (3-volume reissue, 2001)

Poems
*William Carlos Williams; introduction
by Virginia M. Wright-Peterson*
(2002)

Creole Echoes: The Francophone
Poetry of Nineteenth-Century
Louisiana
*Translated by Norman R. Shapiro;
introduction and notes by M. Lynn
Weiss* (2003)

Poetry from *Sojourner: A Feminist Anthology*
Edited by Ruth Lepson with Lynne
    Yamaguchi; introduction by Mary
    Loeffelholz (2004)

Asian American Poetry: The Next
    Generation
*Edited by Victoria M. Chang;
    foreword by Marilyn Chin* (2004)

Papermill: Poems, 1927–35
*Joseph Kalar; edited and with an
    Introduction by Ted Genoways*
    (2005)

The University of Illinois Press
is a founding member of the
Association of American University Presses.

Composed in 10/13.5 ITC Berkeley Oldstyle
by Jim Proefrock
at the University of Illinois Press
Designed by Paula Newcomb
Manufactured by Sheridan Books, Inc.

University of Illinois Press
1325 South Oak Street
Champaign, IL 61820-6903
www.press.uillinois.edu